Desert Workout

LABURNUM
PRESS

Clare Hibbert

LABURNUM PRESS

Laburnum House Educational Ltd
Caldicott Drive
Heapham Road Industrial Estate
Gainsborough
DN21 1FJ

British Library Cataloguing in Publication Data (CIP) exists for this title.

ISBN 9781909850101
Printed by EDELVIVES, Spain
Printed on chlorine-free paper from sustainably managed sources

Developed and Created for Laburnum Press by
White-Thomson Publishing Ltd,
2 St Andrews Place
Lewes, East Sussex, BN7 1UP

Acknowledgements
Educational consultant: Sue Palmer Med FRSA FEA
Project Manager: Katie Dicker
Picture research: Amy Sparks
Design: Balley Design Ltd
Creative director: Simon Balley
Designer/Illustrator: Michelle Tilly/Andrew Li

Contents

In the desert

craggy rocks

Deserts are very dry places.
Most are very hot.

sand

Are you ready to try out some desert moves?

Dunes

step up

Dunes are mountains of sand.

wheeee!

step down

Pretend to march up and down some dunes.

9

Camel train

How many **camels** can you count?

Pretend to take a bumpy camel ride.

Desert peOple

water pot

These women have been to fetch water.

steady! →

How *fast* can you **walk** with something on your *head?*

Scaly Snakes

slither slither

Can you slither like this desert snake?

14

hisssss!

Can you curl up in a coil?

Creepy Crawlies

sting tip

pincer

Lie on your belly and arch your legs to make a **scorpion** shape!

tarantula

Now scuttle like this desert spider!

17

Furry gerbils

Gerbils hop over the hot sand and scamper along underground tunnels.

bo-ing!

You try it!

19

Desert flowers

flap!

cactus plant

At night, bats feed from cactus flowers.

20

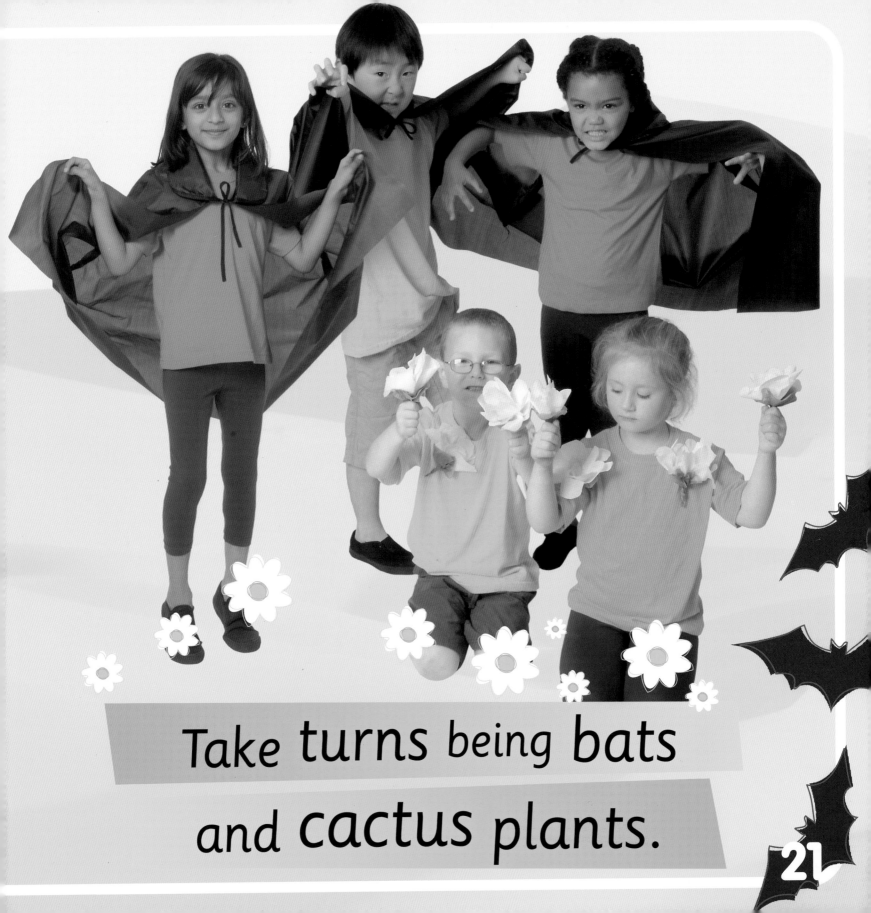

Take turns being bats
and cactus plants.

21

Sparklers books are designed to support and extend the learning of young children. The first four titles in the series won a Practical Pre-School Silver Award. The books' high-interest subjects link in to the Early Years curriculum and beyond. Find out more about Early Years and reading with children from the National Literacy Trust (www.literacytrust.org.uk).

Themed titles

Desert Workout is one of four **Body Moves** titles that explore the animals and climate of a geographic environment, while also stimulating physical activity and role play. The other titles are:

Polar Workout   **Rainforest Workout**   **Underwater Workout**

Areas of learning

Each **Body Moves** title helps to support the following Foundation Stage areas of learning:

Personal, Social and Emotional Development
Communication, Language and Literacy
Mathematical Development
Knowledge and Understanding of the World
Physical Development
Creative Development

If you work with children and want to take a child-led approach to movement, check out JABADAO (www.jabadao.org), who provide training in Developmental Movement Play and supply resources.

Making the most of reading time

When reading with younger children, take time to explore the pictures together. Ask children to find, identify, count or describe different objects. Point out colours and textures. Allow quiet spaces in your reading so that children can ask questions or repeat your words. Try pausing mid-sentence so that children can predict the next word. This sort of participation develops early reading skills.

Follow the words with your finger as you read. The main text is in Infant Sassoon, a clear, friendly font designed for children learning to read and write. The labels and sound effects add fun and give the opportunity to distinguish between levels of communication. Where appropriate, labels, sound effects or main text may be presented phonically. Encourage children to imitate the sounds.

You can also extend children's learning by using the books as a springboard for discussion and further activities. There are a few suggestions on the facing page.

Pages 4–5: In the desert

Make a desert mural, with children's paintings of desert animals on top of a background collage. Help children to look in a reference book or online for a map that shows the world's deserts.

Pages 6–7: Hot sun

Talk to children about keeping safe in hot sun. The middle boy in the picture is drinking water and wearing sunglasses to protect his eyes. Sun cream and a sunhat are essential in the sun, too.

Pages 8–9: Dunes

"The Grand Old Duke of York" is not set in the desert – but it's a great song for children to sing as they march up and down! If you have a slide, children can adapt the activity and climb up, then slide down. Talk to them about how it feels to move in sand, and the difficulties of sinking into it.

Pages 10–11: Camel train

Sing along to "Alice the camel has one hump" – it's an excellent counting song. If you can, let children listen on a CD or online to the sound of camels bellowing, too. Talk to children about the advantages of the clothing worn by the people in the picture on pages 10–11.

Pages 12–13: Desert people

The women carrying water live in India's Thar Desert. Find some Rajasthani folk music to play. If you do not have beanbags, give the children small boxes or unbreakable cartons to balance.

Pages 14–15: Scaly snakes

Children may enjoy pretending to be a snake being charmed, starting out curled up and slowly rising up. Find some pipe music to accompany them. Give children a short length of string so they can mimic the prints left by a desert snake in a sand tray – or dip in paint to make snaky patterns.

Pages 16–17: Creepy crawlies

Encourage children to move their scorpion tail back and forth. They can also shuffle forwards on their elbows. Find a picture of a mother scorpion carrying her babies on her back. The children could go on a treasure hunt as scorpions, collecting as many hidden 'babies' (beanbags) as they can.

Pages 18–19: Furry gerbils

You can set up more equipment for the activity on page 19. Try stepping stones or balance blocks for children to leap between. Give children the opportunity to study a gerbil and exercise their observational skills by visiting a petting zoo or asking someone to bring in their pet.

Pages 20–21: Desert flowers

In this dance activity the 'bats' visit the 'cactus plants' to drink nectar from the flowers. Encourage the cacti to perform expressive hand and arm movements, as if putting forth flowers. Introduce new vocabulary, such as 'flitting' and 'darting', to describe the fast movement of the bats. You can also turn this activity into a collecting game, with something to pick up from each cactus.

Index

Picture acknowledgements:
Alamy: 20 (Rolf Nussbaumer); **Corbis:** 10-11 (Martin Harvey), 18 (DK Limited);
Photolibrary: cover/22-23/24 dunes (Botanica), 2-3/18 (Flirt/Corbis), 12 (Animals Animals/Earth Scenes), 14 (Patricio Robles Gil), 15 (Animals Animals/Earth Scenes), 16 (Animals Animals/Earth Scenes); **Shutterstock:** cover/22-23/24 scene (Paul B. Moore), 4-5 (Gary718), 6-7 (Paul B. Moore), 8-9 (Dainis Derics), 13/21 b/g (Vova Pomortzeff), 17 (Robynrg), 20 (Nathan Chor).

All other photographs by **Simon Punter**.